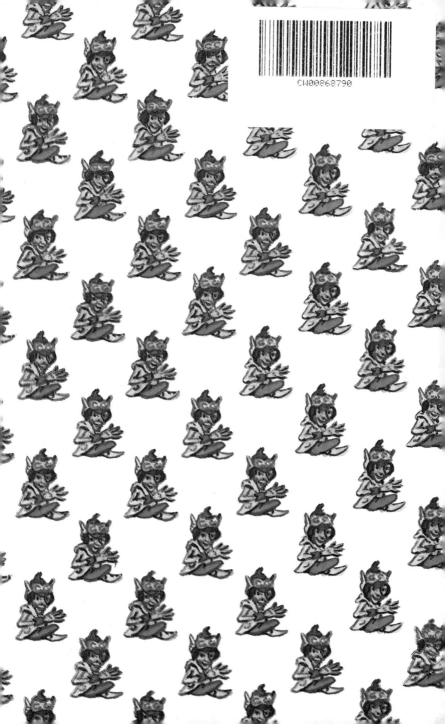

A PUPPY IN WONDERLAND AND OTHER TALES

A Puppy in Wonderland (Previously A Puppy in Fairyland)
Snitty's Lamp Post
The Clockwork Duck

Copyright © Darrell Waters Limited 1951
Copyright © illustrations Century Hutchinson Limited 1986
First published by Pitkin London 1951

Published in 1986 by Hutchinson Children's Books
An imprint of Century Hutchinson Ltd
Brookmount House, 62–65 Chandos Place, Covent Garden,
London WC2N 4NW

Century Hutchinson Publishing Group (Australia) Pty Ltd
16–22 Church Street, Hawthorn, Melbourne, Victoria 3122

Century Hutchinson Group (NZ) Ltd
32–34 View Road, PO Box 40–086, Glenfield, Auckland 10

Century Hutchinson Group (SA) Pty Ltd
PO Box 337, Bergvlei 2012, South Africa

Designed by Sarah Harwood
Edited by Sarah Ware

Set in Souvenir Light 774 12/14pt.
by Southern Positives and Negatives (SPAN), Lingfield, Surrey

Printed and bound in Italy

British Library Cataloguing in Publication Data

Blyton, Enid
        A puppy in wonderland and other tales.
        I. Title   II. Hook, Richard
        823'.912[J]   PZ7

ISBN 0 09 167180 9

Enid Blyton's

A PUPPY
IN WONDERLAND

and other tales

Illustrated by

Richard Hook

Hutchinson

London   Melbourne   Auckland   Johannesburg

A PUPPY IN WONDERLAND

CHIPS was a round, fat little puppy. He belonged to Alan, James and Kate, and they were all very fond of him. He was rather naughty, because he would chew slippers up, and dig great holes in the garden.

'He's a dear little chap,' said Alan, 'but I do wish he'd stop digging in the garden. Daddy is getting so cross!'

'Let's take him for a walk,' said Kate. 'If we make him tired out, he will go to sleep in his basket, and won't get into any more mischief.'

So they called Chips, and he came bounding up to them, delighted to think that he was going for a walk.

'Where shall we go?' asked Alan.

'Through Heyho Wood,' said James. 'It's such a hot day, and it will be nice and cool there.'

So off they started. It was hot! The sun shone down, and there was not a cloud in the sky. They were glad to get into the shady wood.

Chips ran here and there, sniffing at the ground in great excitement. He could smell rabbits! Then he saw one! Oh, my goodness, what a to-do there was! He yelped and barked, and tore off as fast as his short legs would let him, tripping and tumbling over blackberry brambles as he went!

'Chips! Chips! Come here, you'll get lost!' cried Alan.

But Chips took no notice at all. On he went, bounding through the trees, his little tail wagging like mad. He must catch that rabbit, he really must!

But of course he didn't! The rabbit went diving headlong into its hole, and when Chips came up and looked round there was no bunny to be seen!

'It must have gone into the ground like worms do!' thought the puppy. So he chose a nice green place, and began to dig. He scrabbled the earth with his front paws, and sent it flying out behind him with his back ones. He puffed and panted, snorted and sneezed, and he took no notice at all of the shouts and whistles of the children some distance away.

Suddenly there came a shout of rage. Chips looked up in surprise, and what did he see but a brownie, dressed in a brown tunic, long stockings and a pointed hat! He was staring at Chips with a very angry look on his face, and the puppy wondered why. He didn't wonder long, because he suddenly remembered the rabbit again, and once more began to dig madly.

That made the brownie crosser than ever. He took a long green whistle from his pocket and blew seven short blasts on it. Immediately a crowd of little men like himself came up.

'Look!' said the first brownie, fiercely. 'Look at that horrid dog! He's dug a hole right in the very middle of the fairy ring which we got ready for the Queen's dance tonight! And he won't stop, either!'

'Stop! Stop, you naughty dog!' cried all the brownies. 'Stop digging at once!'

But Chips took no notice at all. He just went on digging. The brownies didn't know what to do.

'He may bite if we go too near him,' said one. 'But we must catch him and punish him. Why, the Queen won't be able to have her midnight dance tonight!'

'I know how we can get him!' cried a small brownie. 'Let's go and ask the spiders to give us some of their web! Then we'll throw it round the dog and catch him like that!'

'That's a good idea!' cried all the little men. 'Then we'll take him to prison.'

Chips looked up. He thought the brownies looked very cross indeed. He decided that he would go and find the children. But the brownies had closed round him in a ring, and he could see no way to get through. Then two or three of them came running up with a large net made of sticky spider thread. They suddenly threw it over the puppy – and poor Chips was caught!

He tried to get out of the web, but he couldn't. The brownies dragged him away, and he yelped miserably. The children heard him yelping, and looked at one another.

'Chips is in trouble!' said Kate. 'Quick, come and see what's the matter!'

The three children ran as fast as they could to where they heard the puppy yelping. But when they got there, there was no Chips to be seen. There was only a cross-looking brownie filling in a newly-dug hole.

'Oh!' said the children in surprise, and stopped to look at the funny little man. He looked at them, too, and then went on with his work.

'I suppose you haven't seen our puppy, have you?' asked Kate, at last.

'Oh, so it was your dog, was it?' said the brownie. 'Well, do you know what he has done? Do you see this ring of fine green grass, surrounded by toadstools? It was got ready for a dance tonight, by order of the Queen – and your horrid little dog dug a great big hole in the middle of it. It's all spoilt!'

'Oh dear, I am sorry,' said Alan. 'He really is naughty to do that – but I'm sure he didn't mean any harm. He's only a puppy, you know. He's not four months old yet.'

'Well, he's been taken to prison,' said the brownie. 'He wouldn't even stop when we told him to!'

Kate began to cry. She couldn't bear to think of poor little Chips being taken to prison. Alan put his arm round her.

'Don't worry, Kate,' he said. 'We'll find some way of rescuing him.'

The brownie laughed.

'Oh, no, you won't!' he said. 'We shan't set him free until he's sorry.'

He ran off, and disappeared between the trees. The children stared at one another in dismay.

'We must find Chips!' said Kate. 'Where can they have put him?'

'Look, here are the marks of their footsteps,' said James pointing to where the grass was trodden down. 'Let's follow their tracks as far as we can.'

So they set off. Chips had been carried by the brownies, so they could find no marks of his toes, but they could easily follow the traces left on the long grass by the crowd of brownies.

Through the trees they went, keeping their eyes on the ground. Suddenly the tracks stopped.

'That's funny!' said Alan. 'Where can they all have gone to? Look! They stop quite suddenly just here, in the middle of this little clearing.'

'Perhaps they've flown into the air,' suggested Kate.

'I don't think so,' said Alan. 'That little fellow we met had no wings.'

'Well, did they go down through the ground, then?' wondered James. He looked hard at the grass, and then gave a cry of excitement.

'Look!' he said, 'I do believe there's a trap-door here, with grass growing neatly all over it!'

The children looked down – yes, James was right. There was a square patch there, which might well be a trap-door.

Alan knelt down, and after a few minutes he found out how to lift up the trap-door. James and Kate looked down the opening in excitement. They saw a tiny flight of steps leading into darkness. Alan took out his torch and flashed it into the hole.

'Look!' he cried, and picked up a white hair. 'Here's one of Chips's hairs. Now we know they took him down this way! Come on!'

The three children scrambled down. There were twenty steps, and then a stone platform. To their great astonishment they saw an underground river flowing by.

'Well, Chips must have gone this way because there's no other way for him to go!' said James. 'But how are we to follow! There's no boat to take us.'

But just at that moment a little blue boat floated up, and came to the platform, where it stayed quite still.

'Hurrah!' said Alan. 'Here's just what we want. Come on, you others.'

They all jumped in at once, and the little boat floated away down the dark stream. After a while it came out into the open air, and the children were very glad.

They looked round them in wonder.

'This must be Wonderland!' said Kate. 'Look at all the beautiful castles and palaces!'

'And look at the funny higgledy-piggledy cottages everywhere!' said James.

'And what a crowd of different kinds of fairyfolk!' said Alan. 'Look, brownies, elves, pixies, gnomes, and lots of others!'

'I wonder where the brownies took Chips,' said Kate. 'Shall we ask someone and see if they know?'

'Yes,' said Alan. So they stopped the boat by guiding it gently to the bank, and then asked a passing pixie if he had seen any brownies with a puppy dog.

'Yes,' he said. 'They had him wrapped up in spider's web, and took him to that castle over there.'

He pointed to a castle near-by on a steep hill.

'Thank you,' said Alan. Then he turned to the others. 'Come on,' he said. 'We must leave this boat, and make for the castle,'

Out they all jumped, and took the path that led to the castle. It was not long before they were climbing the hill on which the castle stood. They came to a great gate, and by it hung a bellrope.

Alan pulled it, and at once a jangling noise was heard in the courtyard beyond. The gate swung open, and the children went in, feeling a little bit frightened.

There was no one in the courtyard. Exactly opposite was a door, which stood open. The children went towards it and peeped inside. Just as they got there they heard a sorrowful bark.

'Chips is here!' said Kate, in a whisper. 'Let's go in.'

They crept inside the door, and found themselves in a big hall. At one end was a raised platform on which stood a very grand chair, almost a throne. On it was sitting a very solemn brownie. In front of him, still tied up in the spider's thread, was poor Chips, very much afraid. Round him were scores of little brownies, and they were telling the chief one what he had done.

Kate ran right up to the solemn brownie, and James and Alan followed.

'Please, please let our puppy go!' begged Kate. 'He didn't mean any harm to your fairy ring. He was after a rabbit, that's all.'

'What sort of rabbit?' asked the chief brownie.

'Oh, a big sandy one, with white tips to its ears,' said Alan. 'I saw it just as it ran away from Chips.'

'Then he's a good puppy, not a naughty one!' cried the solemn brownie. 'That rabbit is very bad. It used to draw the Queen's carriage, and what do you think it did?'

'What?' asked the three children.

'Why, one night, it ran away with the carriage and all!' said the brownie. 'The poor Queen was so frightened. The carriage turned over, and she was thrown out. The rabbit ran off, and we have never been able to catch it since.'

'Well, Chips nearly caught it!' said Kate, eagerly. 'And I expect he saw it go into a burrow, and tried to dig it out – only he chose the wrong place, that's all. I'm sure he's very sorry indeed for all the trouble he has caused.'

'Wuff-wuff! Wuff-wuff!' said Chips, sitting up on his back legs, and begging for mercy.

'We'll let him go at once!' cried all the brownies, and two of them ran to cut away the web that bound him. In a trice Chips was free, and danced delightedly round the three children. Kate picked him up and hugged him.

'Take them back to the wood,' commanded the chief brownie. 'And give Chips a bone to make up for his fright.'

The puppy barked in glee when a large bone was given to him. He picked it up in his mouth and began to chew it.

'The carriage is at the door,' said a little brownie, running in. The children were taken to the great door, and outside in the yard stood a grand carriage of silver and gold, driven by a brownie driver. Six small white horses drew the carriage. How excited the children were!

They all got in, said goodbye to the brownies, and then off went the carriage at a smart pace. It went up hill and down dale, through miles of Wonderland, and at last entered the same wood in which their adventures had started that morning.

'Thank you so much,' said the children, as they jumped out. They patted the horses, and then the carriage turned round and was soon out of sight.

The children walked home, and told their mother all that had happened. But she found it very difficult to believe them.

'Are you sure you haven't made it all up?' she asked.

'Well, look, here is the bone that the brownies gave to Chips!' cried Kate. 'And look at his tail! It's still covered with spider's web!'

So it was – and after that their mother had to believe their exciting story, especially as Chips had learnt his lesson, and never, never, never, dug a hole in the garden again!

SNIFTY'S LAMP POST

ONCE upon a time there lived a very disagreeable gnome called Snifty. He was head of the gnome village he lived in, and he was very unkind to everyone.

Now, the Chancellor of Gnomeland came to visit him one night. There was no moon, and it was so dark that the Chancellor could hardly see his way through the village. He drove down the wrong path, and when he got out of his carriage to see where he was, he fell over two or three geese, and then sat down on a frightened pig.

This made him very cross, and when he got to Snifty's house he told him that he ought to be ashamed of having a village which was so dreadfully dark.

'Why don't you have a fine new lamp post put just in front of your house?' he asked. 'Then your visitors would know where you lived, and would not fall over pigs and geese.'

'I will,' said Snifty, rubbing his hands gleefully, glad to think that his villagers would have to buy a fine lamp post for him out of their own money. He didn't once think of buying it himself. He always made his poor people pay for everything, and because they were afraid of him, they did not dare to say no.

So the next day he sent a notice round the village to say that the gnomes were to make him a fine new lamp post.

Then when the Chancellor paid him a call another night he wouldn't go the wrong way.

'Will you give us the money for it?' asked the gnomes.

'Certainly not!' answered Snifty. 'What is the use of being the chief if I can't get things for nothing, I should like to know?'

The gnomes knew that it was of no use to say anything more, but they were very angry.

'It's time we made Snifty stop this sort of thing,' they grumbled. 'He's always expecting us to pay for everything, and he never gives us a penny towards it.'

They began to make the lamp post. It was a lovely one, for the gnomes liked making things as beautiful as they could, no matter whether they were working for people they liked or disliked.

Snifty soon sent them word that the Chancellor was coming to see him again, and he ordered the gnomes to have the lamp post put up in time.

Then the gnomes grumbled even more, and suddenly they decided that they would do just what Snifty said, and no more. They would finish the lamp post and put it up – but they wouldn't put any oil in the lamp, or light it! That would just serve old Snifty right!

So they finished the lamp post and put it up just in front of Snifty's front gate. He watched them from the window, but he didn't bother to come out and say thank you.

The Chancellor arrived that evening, and again it was very, very dark. No one had put any oil in the lamp or lighted it, so there was no light for him to see by again. He was very cross, especially when his carriage got stuck in the ditch and couldn't be moved. He got out, and trod on a hedgehog, which hurt him very much.

'Why doesn't Snifty do as I tell him, and get a lamp post put in front of his gate?' he growled. 'He's rich enough!'

Snifty was very angry when he found that the lamp was not lighted. The Chancellor told him how his carriage had stuck in the ditch, and asked him why it was that he had not got his lamp lighted, to show him the way. Snifty rang a bell, and told his servant to fetch some of the village gnomes, and he would hear why they had disobeyed him.

The gnomes soon came, and Snifty asked them angrily why they had not obeyed him.

'We have obeyed you, Sir,' answered the gnomes. 'You told us to put a lamp post in front of your gate, and we have done so. But you did not tell us to put any oil in it.'

'Oh, you silly, stupid creatures!' cried Snifty, angrily. 'Then hear me now. The Chancellor is coming again tomorrow night, and oil is to be put in the lamp. Do you hear?'

'Yes,' said the gnomes, and went out.

When they had got to their homes they put their heads

together and decided that they would again do exactly as Snifty had said – they would put oil in the lamp, but no wick!

So next day oil was poured into the lamp, but no wick was put in. And when the Chancellor arrived that night he again found that he could not see where Snifty lived! This time he jumped out of his carriage too soon, and walked straight into a very muddy pond. He was so angry when he reached Snifty's at last that he could hardly speak.

Once again Snifty called the gnomes to his house, and asked them what they meant by not obeying him.

'Sir, we have obeyed you,' answered the gnomes. 'We have put oil in the lamp as you bade us. You did not tell us to put in a wick – so how could the lamp be lighted?'

'Then put in a wick' shouted Snifty, very angry indeed.

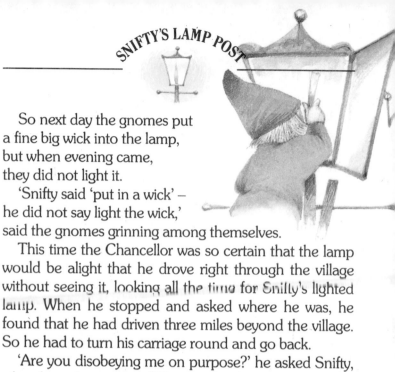

So next day the gnomes put a fine big wick into the lamp, but when evening came, they did not light it.

'Snifty said 'put in a wick' – he did not say light the wick,' said the gnomes grinning among themselves.

This time the Chancellor was so certain that the lamp would be alight that he drove right through the village without seeing it, looking all the time for Snifty's lighted lamp. When he stopped and asked where he was, he found that he had driven three miles beyond the village. So he had to turn his carriage round and go back.

'Are you disobeying me on purpose?' he asked Snifty, when he at last arrived. 'Where is that lamp?'

'Isn't it lighted?' cried Snifty.

'No, it isn't,' answered the Chancellor.

'Then I'll find out why!' cried Snifty in a rage, and he called in the gnomes once more.

'Why have you disobeyed me again?' he shouted angrily.

'We have not disobeyed you!' answered the gnomes in surprise. 'You told us to put a wick in the lamp, and we have done so. We did not hear you order us to light the wick.'

'Then tomorrow light the wick!' roared Snifty.

The gnomes consulted among themselves, and decided that the next night they would light the wick as Snifty had commanded, and then blow it out! So they would be obeying him, and yet he still would not have his light.

They did this. One of them lighted the lamp carefully, and then after five minutes he blew the light out.

Then they waited for the Chancellor to come as usual.

This time the Chancellor was so angry to find that the lamp was again not lighted for him that he almost deafened Snifty with his shouting. Snifty called in the gnomes again, and they explained that he had told them to light the lamp, and they had done so. He had not told them to let it burn all night long, and as oil was expensive they had blown out the light after five minutes.

Snifty was too furious to speak for a whole minute.

'Tomorrow you will light the wick which rests in the oil, and you will see that the lamp is burning all night long,' he cried at last. 'I will have no misunderstanding this time.'

The gnomes went away. For some time they could not think of any way in which they might again trick Snifty, and yet still obey him. Then one of them had a good idea.

'Snifty didn't say anything about where the lamp was to be, did he?' he said. 'Let's move it away from his gate when night comes, and put it somewhere else. We'll light it, and keep it burning all night long – but it won't be in the right place!'

The other gnomes thought this was a splendid idea. So when night came, they went quietly to where the lamp post was, and carried it away to the other end of the village, and there they lighted it.

Very soon the Chancellor came by, and seeing the light, he stopped and got out of his carriage. He was very much puzzled when he could see no sign of Snifty's house. He stopped a little gnome and asked him.

'Oh, Snifty lives at the other end of the village,' answered the gnome.

'Oh dear, oh dear!' said the Chancellor. 'What a nuisance! I have got the King of Gnomeland in my carriage tonight, and I didn't want to lose my way as I usually do. I told Snifty to be sure and have the lamp alight outside his front gate, so that I would know where I was.'

Now when the little gnome heard that the King was in the carriage, he was very much surprised. In a trice he had told the other gnomes, and very quickly they lifted up the lamp post and carried it in front of the carriage to show the driver the way. They set the lamp down by Snifty's front gates, and then cheered the King loudly as he drove by.

'What very nice, good-natured fellows,' said the King, pleased. 'Snifty is lucky to have such fine people in his village.'

When they reached the house, the Chancellor told Snifty that again there had been no lamp outside his house, and sternly asked him why. Snifty gasped with rage, and called in his gnomes at once.

'Why have you disobeyed me again?' he cried.

'We haven't disobeyed,' answered the gnomes. 'You told us to light the lamp, and keep it burning all night long. But you didn't say it was to be outside your gates.'

Then Snifty lost his temper, and said some rude and horrid things to the gnomes in front of the King. The King stopped him and asked to be told all the tale. When he found that night after night Snifty had been tricked over the lamp, he was very much puzzled.

'But your villagers seem such good-natured fellows,' he said. 'Why, they carried the lamp all the way in front of my carriage for me! It is very wrong of them to behave like this. After all, it is your lamp, for you have paid for it, Snifty. They have no right to treat it like that.'

'Excuse me, Your Majesty,' said a gnome, stepping forward. 'We had to pay for the lamp, not Snifty. He makes us pay for everything he wants. If he had paid for the lamp himself, we should not have tried to teach him a lesson.'

'Are you poor?' the King asked Snifty.

'No, Your Majesty,' said Snifty, beginning to tremble.

'Then why do you not pay for your lamp yourself?' asked the King. 'Many tales have reached me lately, Snifty, of your meanness, and I came here to find out if they were true or not. I now see very plainly that they are. Your people were quite right to treat you as you deserve. You must leave the village, and I will make someone else the chief!'

So Snifty had to go, and you may be sure nobody missed him. As for the lamp, it now burns brightly outside the new chief's gates every night, and reminds him to be kind and generous. If he isn't, I don't know what trick the gnomes would play on him – but I'm quite sure they would think of something!

THE CLOCKWORK DUCK

THERE was once a clockwork duck who thought a very great deal of herself. She was made of plastic and floated beautifully. She had a little key in her side, and when she was wound up she paddled herself along in the water.

She lived in the soap dish by the bath, along with the soap, a sponge, a floating goldfish and a little green frog. When Harry had his bath at night the clockwork duck always swam up and down and made him laugh. Mummy used to wind her up, and when she was paddling herself along, the frog and the goldfish, who could only float, thought she was very wonderful indeed.

'You ought to go out on the pond with the real ducks,' said the frog. 'My, wouldn't they think you marvellous.'

'Yes, you are wasted here,' said the goldfish. 'You should go out into the world.'

The clockwork duck listened, and began to long to go out to the real ducks on the pond.

'They would be so proud to have me with them,' she thought. 'Perhaps they would make me their queen! I am very pretty, and when I am wound up I can swim very fast indeed!'

The more she thought about it, the more she wanted to go. And one day, when Spot the dog came into the

bathroom, she called to him and begged him to take her down to the pond in his mouth.

'Very well,' said Spot, in surprise. 'But you'll be sorry you left your nice home in the soap dish, I can tell you! Real ducks haven't any time for clockwork ones!'

He picked up the little duck in his mouth, ran downstairs, went out of the back door, and took the duck to the edge of the pond. He dropped her into the water and left her there.

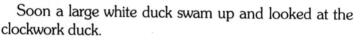

Soon a large white duck swam up and looked at the clockwork duck.

'What are you?' she said.

'A clockwork duck,' said the duck. 'I am a very wonderful duck. I have a key in my side, and when it is wound up I can swim across the water.'

'Well, I can swim over the pond without being wound up at all!' said the other duck. 'I don't think that is very wonderful!'

'You don't know what you are talking about!' said the clockwork duck, crossly. 'You ought to make me queen of the pond, that's what you ought to do! I tell you I am a very marvellous bird!'

By this time other ducks had swum up and were listening to the clockwork duck. Then a frog popped up his green head, and two or three fishes looked out of the water too. The clockwork duck felt that she was making quite a success.

'Wind me up and see how nicely I can swim,' she said.

So a frog swam up to her, took the key in his front fingers and wound her up. Whir-r-r-r, she went, and her legs began to paddle to and fro, sending her quickly over the water.

All the ducks, frogs and fishes laughed to see her, and she was proud to think she had amused them.

'Well,' she said at last, 'would you like to make me your queen?'

'You must prove that you are worthy to be a queen first,' said the big white duck. 'Listen – we big ducks want to swim down the pond and get into the little brook, because we have heard that there is plenty of food to be found in the mud there. But we don't want the little yellow ducklings to go with us.'

'Well, I'll look after them for you, and keep them safe,' said the clockwork duck, proudly. 'Just wind me up once more and I shall be all right.'

So they wound her up, and then swam off to the little brook that ran by the end of the pond. The yellow ducklings swam up to look at the clockwork duck who was to look after them, and when they saw that she was no bigger than they were, they laughed.

'Why, you can't be any older than we are,' they cried. 'We don't want to be looked after by you!'

'You stay with me and be good,' said the clockwork duck, fiercely.

'No,' said the ducklings. 'We want to go after the big ducks and see what food they are finding in the brook. Good-bye!'

With that the naughty little ducklings swam off. The clockwork duck swam after them as fast as she could, but alas! – long before she reached the brook her clockwork ran down, and she could paddle no farther. She could not quack like a real duck, so all she could do was to bob up and down on the ripples, hoping that no harm would come to the yellow ducklings.

Soon she heard a great noise of quacking, and back to the pond came the big ducks with the little ducklings behind them, looking very sorry for themselves.

'What do you mean by letting our ducklings swim off by themselves like that?' quacked the biggest duck, in a temper. 'Do you know that a rat has caught one, and that another got caught in the weeds and couldn't get free!'

'Why didn't you peck them and make them behave?' cried another duck.

'I can't peck,' said the clockwork duck.

'Well, why didn't you swim with them and see that no harm came to them?' shouted a third duck.

'I tried to, but my clockwork ran down, and I couldn't swim any farther,' said the clockwork duck, hanging her head.

'Well, you could have at least have quacked loudly, so

that we should have known something was happening, and could have come to your help!' said the first duck, fiercely.

'But I can't quack!' said the poor clockwork duck.

'Then what use are you!' cried all the ducks, in a rage. 'You're the stupidest, silliest creature we've ever seen, and as for making you our queen, why, we'd sooner ask that dog over there!'

They swam at the frightened duck, and pecked her so hard that little dents came here and there in her plastic skin. Their quacking disturbed Spot the dog, who was lying asleep in the sunshine. He jumped up and ran to the clockwork duck's rescue.

In a trice he picked her up in his mouth and ran off with her.

'Take me back to my nice home in the soap dish,' sobbed the poor little duck. 'I don't like the big outside world.'

So Spot ran upstairs and put her gently back into the soap dish with her good friends the goldfish, the sponge and the soap. They were sorry to hear her sad story.

'Never mind, you shall be our queen!' they said. 'But hush! Here comes Harry for his bath!'

Harry trotted into the bathroom, and Mummy ran the water into the bath. She picked up the clockwork duck and wound her up.

'Oh, Mummy!' cried Harry, in surprise. 'Look how dented and spotted my little duck is! What has done that?'

But Mummy didn't know – and you may be sure that the clockwork duck said never a word!

THE ENID BLYTON TRUST FOR CHILDREN

We hope you have enjoyed these stories. Please think for
a moment about those children who are too ill to do the
exciting things you and your friends do.

Help them by sending a donation, large or small, to the
ENID BLYTON TRUST FOR CHILDREN. The trust will use
all your gifts to help children who are sick or handicapped
and need to be made happy and comfortable.

Please send your postal orders or cheques to:

The Enid Blyton Trust for Children
International House
1 St Katharine's Way
London E1 9UN

Thank you very much for your help